INVESTIGATING FOSSIL FUEL POLLUTION

SUE BRADFORD EDWARDS

Wonder Books
An Imprint of The Child's World®
childsworld.com

The Child's World
childsworld.com

Published by The Child's World®
800-599-READ • www.childsworld.com

Photography Credits
Photographs ©: Shutterstock Images, cover, 2, 9 (turtles), 9 (seagull), 12, 14, 17, 19, 21, 23, 27; Breck P. Kent/Shutterstock Images, 5, 6; Anna Tyukhmeneva/Shutterstock Images, 9 (background); Nikiteev Konstantin/Shutterstock Images, 9 (dolphin); Karina Movsesyan/iStockphoto, 10; Nenad Zivkovic/Shutterstock Images, 13; Vladimir Mulder/Shutterstock Images, 18; Monkey Business Images/Shutterstock Images, 24; Red Line Editorial, 29; iStockphoto, 31

ISBN Information
9781503858060 (Reinforced Library Binding)
9781503860070 (Portable Document Format)
9781503861435 (Online Multi-user eBook)
9781503862791 (Electronic Publication)

LCCN 2021952368

Printed in the United States of America

BRINGING THE WORLD TO YOUNG READERS 1968

ABOUT THE AUTHOR

Sue Bradford Edwards writes nonfiction for young readers from her home in St. Louis, Missouri. She writes about social studies, science, animals, and people.

Fossil fuel pollution harms the environment and human health.

TABLE OF CONTENTS

CHAPTER ONE

OIL SPILLS AND FOSSIL FUEL POLLUTION

A large ship carrying oil floated in the ocean. The ship had struck several rocks. It had not sunk, but oil leaked into the water. If birds swallowed the oil, it could poison them. But if they did not drink the polluted water, the birds could die, because their bodies need water to survive. Shellfish and fish living in shallow water were also at risk.

Cleanup crews hurried to the oil spill. They worked to stop the spread of oil with floating barriers called booms. The booms held the spilled oil in one area. That kept it from reaching shore. The booms protected the rocky beach where seals were sunbathing.

During an oil spill, cleanup crews can use booms to help control the spread of the spilled oil.

Oil spills can be very dangerous for birds.

However, seagulls and pelicans had already landed in the spill. Dozens were coated in oil. Volunteers from a wildlife rescue gathered up the birds and brought them to shore. Then they moved the birds to a cleanup area.

A worker gently held a pelican. She took the bird's temperature and checked to see if it was healthy. A bird with oily feathers is in danger because feathers usually keep the bird warm. But feathers coated in oil can cause a bird to freeze to death.

Although the pelican was oily, it was healthy. The worker took the pelican to the washing room. She lowered the bird into a pool of warm water mixed with dish soap. The soapy water gently swished around the pelican. Once the water in the first pool was oily, the worker took the pelican to another clean pool. When the bird was oil free, it was rinsed. The volunteer used a dryer to dry the bird's feathers. The rescuers kept the pelican for three more days to be make sure it was healthy. Then they took the pelican back to the ocean.

Oil spills happen when ships and **pipelines** carrying oil leak. They also happen where oil is collected, such as oil platforms in the ocean. Oil spills can pollute land or water.

All fossil fuels create pollution. Oil, coal, and natural gas are fossil fuels. They were made from fossils of plants and animals that died millions of years ago. Burning fossil fuels releases energy. This energy can heat buildings, power cars, and light up homes.

There are many types of fossil fuel pollution. Collecting fossil fuels leaves behind unwanted rock and other solid waste. Burning fossil fuels leaves behind ash and other materials that will not burn.

Water can be polluted through oil spills. In addition, water is often used to collect oil and natural gas. Water can also keep machinery cool. All of this water is called wastewater.

When fossil fuels are burned to release energy, they also release a gas called carbon dioxide. Too much carbon dioxide is bad for the Earth. Other tiny particles and waste gases pollute the air. Fortunately, people are working to reduce fossil fuel pollution.

THE DEEPWATER HORIZON OIL SPILL

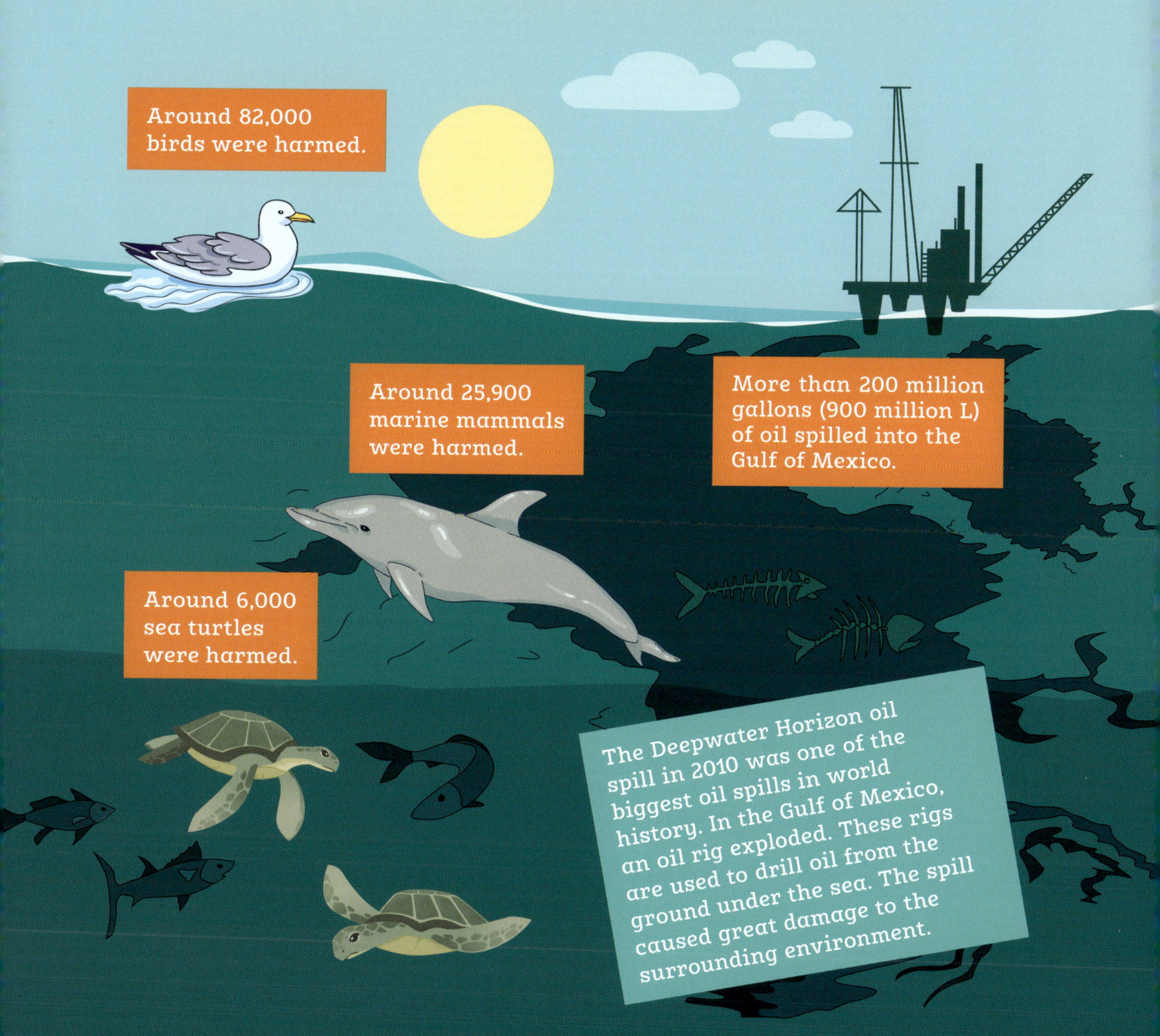

Around 82,000 birds were harmed.

Around 25,900 marine mammals were harmed.

More than 200 million gallons (900 million L) of oil spilled into the Gulf of Mexico.

Around 6,000 sea turtles were harmed.

The Deepwater Horizon oil spill in 2010 was one of the biggest oil spills in world history. In the Gulf of Mexico, an oil rig exploded. These rigs are used to drill oil from the ground under the sea. The spill caused great damage to the surrounding environment.

CHAPTER TWO

SOLID WASTE

Fossil fuels such as coal and oil are mined from the earth. Then they are processed. This creates solid waste.

When people mine for coal, unwanted rock, also known as waste rock, is removed. Waste rock can range in size. It can be as big as a boulder or as small as fine sand. Waste rock is solid waste. After mining, coal is washed with water. Washing coal creates liquid waste called coal sludge. This is also solid waste.

Mined oil can be used to heat up homes and fuel cars and airplanes. However, mining oil negatively affects the environment.

Oil pumped from the earth is not pure. Some **impurities** in the oil pass through filters and are removed. Other times, the oil sits in a tank, and the impurities settle to the bottom of the tank. Sand is one of these impurities. So are metals. These impurities are solid waste.

THE LAND

In addition to creating solid waste, surface coal mining damages the land. Mountaintop removal mines are especially destructive. This is when up to 800 feet (243 m) of mountaintop is removed to get coal. This destroys forests and the soil. When the mine closes, nothing can grow there.

Coal and oil are burned. This leaves behind ash and slag. Slag is a stony material that looks like glass. Ash and slag are also solid waste.

Burning coal creates a large amount of ash. For every 6 tons (5.4 metric tons) of coal that are burned, 1 ton (.9 metric tons) of ash remains. This ash is buried in landfills.

Coal mines add to fossil fuel pollution.

Coal sludge is held in ponds. If the walls containing ponds and landfills break, solid waste is released into the air, water, and soil.

This is dangerous because solid waste is often poisonous. It may contain arsenic, lead, cadmium, and mercury. Arsenic, cadmium, and mercury are metals that can cause cancer. Lead exposure can cause brain damage in children. Mercury is dangerous to fish and the animals that eat the metal. And if a pregnant woman eats the contaminated fish, mercury can hurt her unborn baby.

These toxins make solid waste dangerous to people and to wildlife.

People are trying to reduce solid waste. One way to do this is to find ways to use solid waste. For example, coal ash and slag are used in construction materials. They can also be used to build roads.

Coal ash can even be used to treat piles of solid waste around coal mines. When it rains, water runs off these piles. This runoff is often high in acid and in iron. Rust from this iron turns the water orange. This acidic water is poisonous to plants and animals that live in streams and rivers. Coal ash can **neutralize** the acid and keep solid waste from polluting water.

Coal ash can be reused. However, coal ash is more often thrown away in landfills, which causes environmental damage.

CHAPTER THREE

WATER POLLUTION

Fossil fuel pollution can affect bodies of water. On October 1, 2021, an oil spill was discovered off California's coast. The US Coast Guard believed a ship's anchor struck an underwater pipeline. The pipeline may have been struck many times. When the pipeline cracked, thousands of gallons of oil leaked into the ocean. Cleanup crews found dozens of dead birds. They recovered 5,500 gallons (2,800 L) of oil. Oil was even found 50 miles (80 km) away from the leak.

Oil spills can happen when boats crash, pipes burst, or equipment breaks.

TOO MUCH WATER

Fracking does not only lead to pollution. It also uses a lot of water. Scientists at Duke University studied fracking in the Permian Basin in West Texas. They found that the average fracking job used 10.5 million gallons (40.7 million L) of water. The land was experiencing a drought, and fracking made water even scarcer.

Fracking also pollutes water. Fracking is when a fluid is blasted deep underground to fracture, or break, rocks that hold fossil fuels such as oil and natural gas. When the oil or natural gas is released, they can be pumped to the surface. The fracking fluid is often made up of acids that can dissolve rock. Many of these chemicals are poisonous. After fracking fluid is used, it is stored in pits and pumped into old oil wells. It is moved from place to place in pipelines. But when these pipelines leak, fracking fluid pollutes land and water.

Water is used to help make electricity. Many power plants burn coal, natural gas, or oil. Other power plants use **nuclear energy**. Water is heated into steam that turns machines called turbines. These turbines produce electricity. Then water is used to cool the steam. The cheapest way to do this is to draw water from a lake or river. As the water cools the steam, the water heats up. The heated water is returned to the lake or river. In the United States, 43 percent of all power plants use this method.

The water that is used to cool steam may have chemicals added to it. These chemicals help keep the water from destroying pipes. One of these chemicals is called hydrazine. This chemical can cause cancer.

Water is important to nuclear power plants. Most power plants are near bodies of water.

The temperature of the water can also be a problem. If the water is too hot, it raises the temperature of the river or lake. Warmer water holds less oxygen, so fish that live in the water sometimes die. Pollution caused by the release of hot water is called thermal pollution.

Pipes carry water to cool down power plants.

People are working to reduce the amount of water used to make electricity. One way to do this is to reuse the water that cools the steam. The water can be cooled in ponds and reused. Some power plants use air instead of water. Both methods are more expensive, but they reduce water use by 90 percent.

CHAPTER FOUR

AIR POLLUTION

Air pollution is another problem. Fossil fuels cause several types of air pollution. Natural gas does not spill the way oil can. Instead, natural gas leaks. Leaks can occur where natural gas is taken from the ground or where the gas is processed. Pipelines can leak. So can valves where natural gas goes into homes. Gas meters that measure the amount of gas a household uses can also leak. Hot water heaters, furnaces, stoves, and clothes dryers that burn natural gas can leak, too.

When gas meters leak gas, they can explode.

Natural gas is mostly methane. Methane is a **greenhouse gas**. Greenhouse gases trap heat in Earth's **atmosphere**. That contributes to **climate change**. Only one other greenhouse gas is worse than methane. That gas is carbon dioxide. It is one of the waste gases left behind when fossil fuels are burned. This means that burning fossil fuels also contributes to climate change.

Climate change causes rising temperatures and changing weather patterns. Changing weather leads to less rain in some areas. It can lead to flooding in others. Temperatures rise and polar ice melts. That causes sea levels to rise. All of this puts people and wildlife at risk.

In addition to waste gases, tiny particles are left behind when fossil fuels are burned. This air pollution can harm people's health. It is especially dangerous to children and the elderly. People with other health problems can also get sick from these particles. Some of these particles are larger than others.

Burning fossil fuels affects air quality, which can lead to health issues.

The tiny particles can cause sinus infections and respiratory infections. Small particles move deeper into the lungs. They can cause heart attacks, asthma, and strokes. Adults who breathe in these particles may develop heart or lung diseases. The particles can even slow down brain development.

ACID RAIN

Sulfur dioxide is found in fossil fuel air pollution. When it combines with rain, the rain is more acidic than normal. It is known as acid rain. Frogs and fish can be harmed by acid rain. It can also damage stone buildings.

People are working to improve air pollution problems that are caused by burning fossil fuels. One way to help is by using smokestack scrubbers. Scrubbers make the smoke coming out of a power plant cleaner. Many of these scrubbers filter out sulfur dioxide, which is a gas that can harm the environment.

Driving electric cars can be better for the environment than driving cars fueled by gasoline.

Another way to improve air pollution from fossil fuels is by changing which energy people use. For example, driving electric cars creates less air pollution than cars that use gasoline. Using wind, sun, and water to make electricity reduces the use of fossil fuels.

People can take simple steps to use less energy. They can start by keeping their homes warmer in summer and cooler in winter. This keeps their air conditioners and heaters from running as often.

CHAPTER FIVE

SOLVING THE PROBLEM

Fossil fuel pollution damages the land, air, and water. It harms plants, animals, and people. Fortunately, there are things people can do to fight this pollution.

The easiest thing to do is to use less energy. People can start by turning off lights when they leave rooms. Turning off the television and fans helps, too. If the heat or air conditioning is on, make sure no windows are open. Instead of turning up the heat during the winter, people can wear warm clothes. In the summer, people can turn on the air conditioner only when it is really hot.

Electricity used in people's homes is called residential electricity. In 2020, 31 percent of all residential electricity was used for heating and cooling.

Another way to reduce fossil fuel pollution is to use green energy. Fossil fuels are nonrenewable. This means that once the fossil fuel has been used up, it is gone. The sun, wind, and water are sources of renewable energy. The energy these things create is sometimes called green energy. Green energy creates much less pollution. Some families can use green energy. People can use solar chargers for their cell phones. They can also make electricity by installing solar panels outside. Cities can use wind turbines, which use the wind to make electricity.

People can also save energy as they move from place to place. One way is to carpool. For example, instead of each student driving to school, a couple of students can ride together.

Riding bikes instead of riding in a car can help reduce fossil fuel pollution.

Public transportation is another option. Some areas have subway stations. Other areas have buses. People can also bike or walk.

Another way to reduce fossil fuel pollution is for people to write to their Congress members. These are the people who make decisions about energy. The letters can encourage people in Congress to support alternative energy sources. Fossil fuel pollution is serious. But there are things everyone can do to help.

FAST FACTS

- Coal, natural gas, and oil are fossil fuels. People burn them to release energy. Fossil fuels create pollution.
- Mining and processing coal creates solid waste pollution in the form of waste rock and sludge.
- Filtering oil and burning coal also create solid waste.
- Coal ash and slag are forms of solid waste that can be used in cement and concrete. Coal ash is also used to neutralize the acids and iron in waste rock piles around coal mines.
- Oil spills are a form of water pollution. They harm the water and wildlife.
- Natural gas leaks release methane into the air. Methane is a greenhouse gas. It contributes to climate change. Carbon dioxide is another greenhouse gas. It is produced when fossil fuels are burned.
- People can help fight pollution by using less electricity, using green energy, and writing to their Congress members.

OIL SPILL

MATERIALS

- 2 clear cups or jars
- Water
- Rocks or gravel
- Vegetable oil
- Measuring tablespoon

DIRECTIONS

1. Add water to the first jar. Fill it about halfway. Now pour about 2 tablespoons of vegetable oil onto the water.

   What happens to the oil? What would happen if an animal tried to drink the water? What about if a bird tried to land on the water?

2. Add rocks or gravel to the second jar. Fill it about halfway. Now pour about two tablespoons of vegetable oil onto the rocks or gravel.

   Watch what happens to the oil. Does it stay on top of the rocks? How easy do you think it would be to clean up the oil?

GLOSSARY

atmosphere (AT-muhs-feer) An atmosphere is the layers of gases that surround a planet. Greenhouse gases can damage the atmosphere.

climate change (KLY-mit CHAYNJ) Climate change refers to long-term changes in global temperatures. Climate change causes problems for wildlife habitats.

greenhouse gas (GREEN-howss GAS) A greenhouse gas traps heat in Earth's atmosphere. Methane is a greenhouse gas.

impurities (im-PYOOR-i-tees) Impurities are unwanted particles that contaminate what they are in. Impurities must be filtered out of oil.

neutralize (NOO-truh-lyz) Neutralize means to make something ineffective. Toothpastes neutralize the acid that causes teeth to decay.

nuclear energy (NOO-klee-ur EN-ur-jee) Nuclear energy is created when atoms split apart. People use nuclear energy to get electricity.

pipelines (PIPE-lines) Pipelines are long series of pipes. Pipelines are used to transport oil and fracking fluid across the country.

WAYS YOU CAN HELP

- Participate in your school's science fair. You can do your project on solar or wind energy. With your project, you can educate people on better energy alternatives to fossil fuels.
- Carpool with your friends to school. This can help reduce the use of gasoline.
- Ask your parents to help you find the names of your senators and representatives. Write letters to these people about reducing the use of fossil fuel energy.

FIND OUT MORE

In the Library

Clark, Stacy. *Planet Power: Explore the World's Renewable Energy.* Concord, MA: Barefoot Books, 2021.

MacCarald, Clara. *Investigating Nuclear Pollution.* Mankato, MN: The Child's World, 2023.

Wang, Andrea. *How Can We Reduce Fossil Fuel Pollution?* Minneapolis, MN: Lerner, 2016.

On the Web

Visit our website for links about investigating fossil fuel pollution: **childsworld.com/links**

Note to Parents, Teachers, and Librarians: We routinely verify our Web links to make sure they are safe and active sites. So encourage your readers to check them out!

INDEX